ABIDING HOPE

ABIDING HOPE

Abiding: continuing without
change; enduring; steadfast

Hope: the feeling that what is
wanted can be had or that events
will turn out for the best

T. Windahl

TRISTAN Publishing
Minneapolis

Library of Congress Cataloging-in-Publication Data

Name: Windahl, Tamara, author.
Title: Abiding hope / written by Tamara Windahl.
Description: Minneapolis : TRISTAN Publishing, 2016.
Identifiers: LCCN 2016020168 | ISBN 9781939881106 (alk. paper)
Subjects: LCSH: Cancer--Religious aspects--Christianity--Meditations. |
  Cancer--Patients--Religious life.
Classification: LCC BV4910.33 .W55 2016 | DDC 248.8/6196994--dc23 LC record
available at https://lccn.loc.gov/2016020168

abiding. Dictionary.com. Dictionary.com Unabridged. Random House, Inc. http://www.dictionary.com/browse/abiding(accessed: September 8, 2016).

hope. Dictionary.com. Dictionary.com Unabridged. Random House, Inc. http://www.dictionary.com/browse/hope(accessed: September 8, 2016).

Photograph by Kelly McClintock

TRISTAN Publishing, Inc.
2355 Louisiana Avenue North
Golden Valley, MN 55427

Copyright © 2016, T. Windahl
ISBN 978-1-939881-10-6
First Printing
Printed in Canada

To learn about all of our books with a message, please visit
www.TRISTANpublishing.com

To the One who rescued me,

healed me and taught me

how to walk through the fire.

The glory belongs to you!

T.

FOREWORD

I know "T" and her family personally, and I can tell you they "get it." This family loves Jesus Christ and His church! The dilemma of suffering and God's sovereignty is the backdrop for T's book, *Abiding Hope*. And she doesn't write "theoretically." T has suffered. In a ten-year stretch of her life, she battled four separate cancer diagnoses—including stage-four ovarian cancer; so she is a trusted guide on these matters. In her book you'll find biblically sound insights—including life lessons that will help you through your own pain and suffering.

Read this book and be inspired.

Read this book and be encouraged.

Read this book and be hopeful again.

Pastor Troy Dobbs
Senior Pastor, Grace Church

INTRODUCTION

We live in a world that often tries to rob us of hope! Horrible events are happening around us with greater frequency and greater intensity.

As we survey the landscape of this time and place, as well as the landscape of our own lives, it would be easy to give up and instead live in hopelessness and fear. Thankfully, this isn't our only choice! Abiding hope—hope that is permanent, enduring and continuing without change—is possible! And I learned this truth amidst the fiery circumstances of my own life.

As those close to me know, I have been *through the fire* many times in my life, and those fires make a long list: a cross-country move as a newlywed, which meant leaving friends and family behind; a job loss for my husband; trouble conceiving a baby; a miscarriage; marital problems resulting from a party lifestyle; and four separate cancer diagnoses within ten years—*beginning* with stage-four ovarian cancer in 1991. At times, the fires have raged!

Although I've endured and survived many fires in my life, I seldom replay them in my mind. Instead I choose to consider the good that has come from my suffering, including the many lessons learned!

In the following pages I will share with you where I turned for help, along with some of the lessons I have learned within my most difficult trials. What I discovered within those circumstances changed my life forever and also helped me to become better instead of bitter.

I have learned that no matter what kind of fire is raging, abiding hope is always possible—no matter who we are or what type of fire is raging around us . . . or in us.

Don't worry about anything; instead, pray about everything; tell God your needs, and don't forget to thank him for his answers. If you do this, you will experience God's peace, which is far more wonderful than the human mind can understand. His peace will keep your thoughts and your hearts quiet and at rest as you trust in Christ Jesus.

(Philippians 4:6–7, TLB)

WORRY OR PRAY?

In 1991, a friend gave me a copy of *The Living Bible*. At the time I was an unbeliever, a partyer, a young wife and mom—and I had just been diagnosed with stage-four ovarian cancer. Following that devastating diagnosis, fear and worry came knocking; and I let them in daily, not knowing that I had a choice. But one day, after repenting of my sins and trusting in Jesus, I happened to read Philippians 4:6–7 in the Bible my friend had given me. It was one of the passages she had highlighted for me in pink, "Don't worry about anything; instead, pray about everything; tell God your needs, and don't forget to thank him for his answers. If you do this, you will experience God's peace, which is far more wonderful than the human mind can understand. His peace will keep your thoughts and your hearts quiet and at rest as you trust in Christ Jesus." After reading those verses, I realized that I did have a choice. I could either pray about everything or worry about everything. It was then that I began to apply Philippians 4:6 in my life. When fearful and worrisome thoughts came to mind, I chose to pray instead of worrying. When I did that, I found Philippians 4:7 fleshed out in my life—God's peace entered in . . . the fearful and worrisome thoughts sent packing! When worrisome or fearful thoughts come knocking, we don't have to let them in! For believers in Jesus, God's peace is there for the taking when we stop worrying and pray instead. So what about you? Like me, will you choose to pray about everything instead of worrying about everything? God's peace awaits you if you do . . . the peace that transcends all understanding. And God's peace is one of the greatest gifts he gives to his children . . . especially during hard times. Pray or worry? The choice is ours . . . today and every day.

Lift up your eyes and look to the heavens: Who created all these? He who brings out the starry host one by one and calls forth each of them by name. Because of his great power and mighty strength, not one of them is missing.

(Isaiah 40:26)

HE CALLS THEM EACH BY NAME!

Isaiah 40 is one of my favorite passages to ponder when hard times hit. Why? Because in that chapter, we get a mind-blowing glimpse of the greatness of our God! For some examples of that greatness, check out these verses:

Verse 12 - Who has measured the waters in the hollow of his hand, or with the breadth of his hand marked off the heavens? Who has held the dust of the earth in a basket, or weighed the mountains on the scales and the hills in a balance?

Verse 15 - Surely the nations are like a drop in a bucket; they are regarded as dust on the scales; he weighs the islands as though they were fine dust.

Verse 26 - Lift up your eyes and look to the heavens: Who created all these? He who brings out the starry host one by one and calls forth each of them by name. Because of his great power and mighty strength, not one of them is missing.

As you consider your own life today, are you struggling amidst an impossible situation? If so, I encourage you to ponder Isaiah 40. And with verse 26 fresh on your mind, I also encourage you to think of a night sky filled with stars. Or better yet, if it's nighttime right now—as you're reading this—go outside and look up! Then let those stars remind you of God . . . the One who brings out the starry host one by one and calls them each by name. Finally, give your difficult and impossible situation to God and ask for his help, for nothing is impossible for him! Remember the stars? He calls them each by name! All-powerful and mighty is he!

"I do believe!

Help my unbelief."

(Mark 9:24, HCSB)

HELP MY UNBELIEF

In Mark 9 we find the story of a father whose son had been possessed by an evil spirit since childhood. Desperate, the father had taken his son to Jesus' disciples, but they were unable to cast out the demon. When Jesus arrived on the scene, the father shared that fact with Jesus and said to him, "'But if You can do anything, have compassion on us and help us.' Then Jesus said to him, "'If You can'? Everything is possible to the one who believes'" (verses 22–23). Upon hearing those words, the father immediately realized he needed more faith and cried out to Jesus, "I do believe! Help my unbelief." Jesus then cast the evil spirit out of his son. Jesus didn't just cast out an evil spirit from a son that day, though. He also cast out shackles of unbelief from a father's desperate heart . . . unbelief that had been forged in the fires of difficult circumstances. Are there areas of unbelief in your life today? Unbelief that has been forged in the fires of your difficult life circumstances? If so, then I encourage you to do as the father in Mark 9 did. Cry out to Jesus, *Lord, I do believe! Help my unbelief,*" for "everything is possible to the one who believes."

"It is because God has made me fruitful

in the land of my suffering."

(Genesis 41:52)

SUFFERING AND FRUIT

Years ago I attended a funeral where the "spiritual leader" told those gathered, "There is no purpose for our suffering." I immediately recognized his words as a lie, for God clearly tells us in the Bible that there *is* a purpose for our suffering! (See Romans 5:3–4, James 1:2–4, 1 Peter 1:6–7 and Psalms 119:67.) Thinking about suffering and purpose, I'm reminded of Joseph's story in Genesis. He was betrayed by his brothers, falsely accused of rape, imprisoned, and forgotten by others whom he had helped. After his release from prison though, he was promoted to Prime Minister of Egypt . . . a position through which God used Joseph to save his family—and even his nation—from famine. Later in the story, Joseph told his brothers, who had betrayed him, "You intended to harm me, but God intended it for good to accomplish what is now being done, the saving of many lives" (Genesis 50:20). Also, when Joseph named his second son Ephraim, he said, "It is because God has made me fruitful in the land of my suffering." How encouraging to know that God can use our suffering for good and can make us fruitful in the land of our suffering! As God's children, we may not always understand God's ways in our lives, but if we choose to trust him, he *will* bring fruit out of our suffering. His purposes will be accomplished. Will you choose to trust God in your affliction today? He has a harvest in mind, and that harvest is bigger than you can even imagine! So don't give up . . . trust God. Fruit is on the way!

"Can a mother forget the baby at her breast and have no compassion on the child she has borne? Though she may forget, I will not forget you! See, I have engraved you on the palms of my hands."

(Isaiah 49:15–16)

NOT FORGOTTEN BY GOD

During my first cancer experience, I felt forgotten by two of our closest friends. Prior to my diagnosis, we had gotten together weekly with those friends; but after cancer struck, we never heard from them again. It's hard to be forgotten by friends. It's even harder to feel forgotten by God, though; and during times of suffering, it's easy to feel that way. If we ever feel forgotten by God, we need to remember the following truth found in Isaiah 49:15: "Can a mother forget the baby at her breast and have no compassion on the child she has borne? Though she may forget, I will not forget you!" In that verse from Isaiah, God promised his people that he would not forget them; and down through the ages, that same promise has encouraged countless believers, including myself, time and again. At the cross, we were engraved on the palms of Jesus' hands, and God will not forget us. Our feelings may try to convince us otherwise, but our feelings can lie! A chorus from one of my favorite songs reminds me that I am not forgotten and that God knows my name. God has not forgotten you either, and he knows your name, too! Yes, others may forget us . . . but not God! He will never forget us! Hebrews 13:5 promises that he will never leave us either. So when you find your life's boat being rocked by the wind and waves of difficult trials, strap on the following life jackets, for starters, to keep you from drowning in despair: Isaiah 49:15–16 and Hebrews 13:5. The wind and the waves of difficult circumstances are no match for the truth of God's Word. His Word will help keep you afloat . . . no matter the size of the wave . . . no matter the length of the storm.

He is despised and rejected by men,
a Man of sorrows and acquainted with grief.
(Isaiah 53:3, NKJV)

JESUS UNDERSTANDS

Long before Jesus came to earth as God in the flesh, completely human and completely divine (Colossians 2:9), Isaiah painted a portrait of him in Isaiah chapter 53. In that passage, we see the foreshadowed suffering and death of the suffering servant, Jesus. I have read that chapter and heard verses quoted from it countless times, but on one particular day, part of verse 3 stood out to me like never before: "a Man of sorrows and acquainted with grief." Jesus, the Savior of the world, God's one and only sinless Son, was "a Man of sorrows and acquainted with grief." Upon coming to earth, Jesus entered into the human experience. Not just an onlooker, Jesus personally experienced sorrow, grief and pain. Think about it . . . Jesus was despised, rejected, betrayed, flogged, humiliated and, finally, crucified. Who better than he to come alongside us and comfort us in our sorrow? Who better to understand our pain and grief? On the day this verse first stood out to me, my husband and I visited our friend Joe at a hospice center; and with Isaiah 53:3 fresh on my mind, I shared it with Joe. I prayed those words would stay with Joe daily . . . to remind him that his Savior understands what he was going through. For Jesus has known unimaginable pain and sorrow himself. When no one else understands the pain you're going through, Jesus can. For he is "a Man of sorrows and acquainted with grief." Cry out to him today.

*T*hen Jesus said, "Did I not tell you that if you

believe, you will see the glory of God?"

(John 11:40)

BELIEVE AND SEE

A few years ago in a Bible study, I was asked, "Have you experienced some special benefit of trusting God?" Believe me, I couldn't stop at just one benefit so I listed all of the following: peace and joy amidst difficult circumstances, much answered prayer, clear guidance from God, seeing God's higher and better plans for my life unfold instead of my own puny plans . . . and more. Back then, after I pondered that Bible study question into the night, John 11:40 came to mind, "Then Jesus said, 'Did I not tell you that if you believe, you will see the glory of God?'" As soon as I considered those words, I realized it contained another benefit of trusting God. We get to see his glory! I realized then that, for me, seeing God's glory had to be the greatest benefit of trusting God! By believing God, I have seen God's glory. I have also seen his power. I chose to believe God and his words to me early on in my cancer journey; and if I hadn't, I would have missed seeing his glory and power! Sometimes it takes everything within us to believe God and his words to us, but when we choose to believe God, He chooses to reveal himself to us. And trust me . . . you don't want to miss seeing him! Nothing else in all the world compares with that! So what can you believe God for today? Or what can you continue to believe God for? Got it? Now let the same words Jesus originally spoke to Mary of Bethany fall fresh from heaven to you: "Then Jesus said, 'Did I not tell you that if you believe, you will see the glory of God?'" Believe and see!

Those who sow with tears will

reap with songs of joy.

(Psalm 126:5)

SOWING GOD'S WORD

A few years ago, I heard a Bible teacher say that, when we're going through a hard time, we need to sow God's Word into our circumstances (based on Psalm 126:5 and Matthew 13:3–9). After hearing those words and pondering them in light of my cancer journey, I realized that this was exactly what I had done. Even on the days that were wrapped in tears, I continued sowing seeds of God's Word into the soil of my circumstances. For example, while looking in the mirror back in 1992 and seeing a gaunt, ninety-pound, 5-foot-7½-inch woman staring back at me, I used to say—either in my mind or aloud—this seed from God's Word (a promise that God had personally given to me back then): "But those who wait for the Lord shall renew their strength, they shall mount up with wings like eagles, they shall run and not be weary, they shall walk and not faint" (Isaiah 40:31, NRSV). Day after day I continued believing God and applying his Word to my circumstances. What happens though, when the sowing season drags on for us, and our hard times never seem to end? We continue sowing. We continue trusting God, for as believers, we are promised a harvest...a harvest of joy! What have you been sowing into your hard circumstances lately? A negative attitude? A complaining spirit? If so, choose instead to start sowing God's Word. The Bible is full of seeds for sowing. For starters, check these out:

Luke 1:37, NRSV - "For nothing will be impossible with God."

Isaiah 49:15 - "Can a mother forget the baby at her breast and have no compassion on the child she has borne? Though she may forget, I will not forget you!"

Jeremiah 29:11 -"For I know the plans I have for you," declares the Lord, "plans to prosper you and not to harm you, plans to give you hope and a future."

Plant some seeds from God's Word today and know that one day you will reap a harvest. A good harvest . . . a harvest worth waiting for! "Those who sow with tears will reap with songs of joy."

Cast your burden on the LORD,

and he will sustain you;

he will never permit

the righteous to be moved.

(Psalm 55:22, NRSV)

CAST YOUR BURDEN

Years ago I received a devastating phone call from a dear friend who told me that Robbie, one of our neighbors during my growing up years, had been killed. A truck had run into his sightseeing bus in Africa. Robbie was just twenty-five years old. Upon hearing that horrible news, I cried uncontrollably and eventually called Robbie's parents. Later, in bed, I prayed and reached for my Bible, hoping to find comfort; yet nothing I read seemed to speak to me personally. But when I placed my Bible back on the nightstand, out fell a slip of paper. On the paper was written a verse: Psalm 55:22. I quickly turned to that verse in my Bible and read, "Cast your burden on the LORD, and he will sustain you; he will never permit the righteous to be moved." After reading those words, I was speechless. I sensed the Lord drawing near to instruct and comfort me. Years later I learned that the original Hebrew word for *cast* means "to throw, hurl or fling." Sometimes when I pray, I imagine physically casting my burdens . . . throwing them, hurling them, flinging them . . . upon God; and when I choose to cast my burdens on God, he promises to sustain me. The original Hebrew word for *sustain* has also been translated as "support, maintain, nourish and hold." Think on that as you read Psalm 55:22 again. We cast. God sustains. What a promise! What a God! Today may you "cast your burden on the LORD and he will sustain you; he will never permit the righteous to be moved." Praise be to God!

Set your minds on things above,

not on earthly things.

(Colossians 3:2)

SETTING OUR MINDS ON THINGS ABOVE

Years ago on the cancer journey, God taught me to set my mind on things above instead of on earthly things. What did that look like in my life? While my doctors, nurses and others around me focused on the cancer, I chose not to. Instead, my main focus each day was on God and his Word. While attending to earthly responsibilities, I often pondered who God is according to his Word (not according to other people's words) . . . all-powerful, good, loving, forgiving, compassionate, merciful, faithful and more. I also contemplated encouraging Bible verses for my situation and listened to and sang worship songs, which reminded me that God is above *all* things. Plus, I considered story after story of Jesus healing the sick. Back then I chose to set my mind on spiritual things (still do!), and by doing that, I was reminded that nothing is impossible with God, that my difficult circumstances wouldn't last forever, that God was in control no matter what and that God was at work for good in my situation. Our circumstances can scream for attention 24/7, but we can choose to focus on the things unseen. When we as believers do that, God's peace will be ours; and hope will spring up. Even during good times, God wants us to set our minds on eternal realities. Why? So we don't waste all our time on the earthly, the temporary . . . the things that have no eternal value. For God knows that the things above . . . the things unseen . . . are the greater reality. Where is your focus today? On spiritual things? Or on earthly things? "Set your minds on things above, not on earthly things." Need help? For starters, I encourage you to ask God for his help in obeying Colossians 3:2, and then check out Isaiah 40:6–31. A focus on things above can make all the difference in our days—in our lives—in the good times as well as in the hard.

But he said to me, "My grace is sufficient for you, for my power is made perfect in weakness." Therefore I will boast all the more gladly about my weaknesses, so that Christ's power may rest on me.

(2 Corinthians 12:9)

GOD'S GRACE

One facet of God's grace is that it allows us to do what we could never do on our own. For example, in my own life, God's grace has enabled me to go through four bouts with cancer. Looking back on my cancer journey, I recall a certain memory. Psalm 84:11 tells us that "the Lord gives grace" (HCSB). During my second cancer, he did so in an amazing way. My radiation nurse's name was Grace. I saw her every day of my radiation treatments; and when I did, I was reminded that grace would see me through. How did that happen? God's grace helped me to persevere through those days of radiation and a second round of chemo. His grace enabled me to think of others when I was suffering myself. God's grace also helped me to continue trusting him, even when I didn't understand his ways. Daily I cried out to him for grace, and he saw me through! Back then I learned the importance of grace, and I still pray daily for God's grace for myself and my family. Here's one final word about grace. As believers depending on God, we receive God's grace right when we need it. It's never early, and it's never late. How about you? Where do you need God's grace today? At home? At work? In your marriage? Amidst devastating news? While raising children? Cry out to God when you need grace for any situation, for his grace is sufficient in any circumstance, and it's only a prayer away! "My grace is sufficient for you, for my power is made perfect in weakness."

The LORD *is my rock, my fortress and my deliverer;*
my God is my rock, in whom I take refuge, my shield
and the horn of my salvation, my stronghold.

(Psalm 18:2)

GOD, OUR DELIVERER

In Psalm 18, David refers to God as "my deliverer." David not only knew that God delivers, but through his life experiences, David had come to know God as his *personal* deliverer. Thinking about that fact, I'm reminded of one morning, years ago, when I was headed to the hospital for surgery. While I was driving out of our neighborhood, a song interrupted my thoughts. It was a song that I had heard performed by a children's choir just days before. The message of the song is that our deliverer is coming and that he is standing by. What encouragement that song was to me on my way to surgery! It reminded me that—at that very moment— God, my deliverer, *was* coming and that he *was* standing by. Like David, I have come to know God as *my* deliverer . . . through *my* life experiences. He is the one who has delivered me from cancer, from fear, from myself and my own selfish desires, from a negative attitude, from condemnation, from shame and from so much more! He is the God who delivers, and he is my deliverer. Are you in need of a deliverer today? If so, cry out to God. He is able to deliver. "The LORD is my rock, my fortress and my deliverer." And nothing is impossible for him!

"I will never leave you nor forsake you."

(Joshua 1:5)

NEVER FORSAKEN

Pondering Joshua 1:5 has strengthened me many times during the storms of my life. God promises in that verse that he will never leave or forsake one of his own, and Psalm 145:13 tells us that God is faithful to his promises. Though others may not fulfill their promises, God always does. What God promises, God delivers. Though others may lie to us, God won't. In fact, Numbers 23:19 says this: "God is not human, that he should lie, not a human being, that he should change his mind. Does he speak and then not act? Does he promise and not fulfill?" Though others may leave or forsake us, God never will. God is God . . . not just another one of us. When you find yourself in the middle of a storm, let the words of Joshua comfort you . . . "I will never leave you nor forsake you." If you are a child of God, you are not alone. God is there. God is there.

"He will wipe every tear from their eyes. There will be no more death' or mourning or crying or pain, for the old order of things has passed away."

(Revelation 21:4)

OUR STRUGGLES ARE TEMPORARY

Chapter 21 of Revelation, the last book of the Bible, tells us that one day there will be a new heaven and a new earth where God will dwell among his people. It will be a place where there will be no more death or mourning or crying or pain. It's hard to imagine such a place while living in this world . . . a world full of physical pain, emotional pain, sorrow and death. Revelation 21:4 is one of my favorite verses, and it's a verse that fills me with hope every time I read it! Why? Because it reminds me that the best is yet to come and that the struggles I'm going through here on earth are temporary! So amidst the struggles you may be enduring today, remember the words of Revelation 21:4: "He will wipe every tear from their eyes. There will be no more death' or mourning or crying or pain, for the old order of things has passed away." If you are a child of God, the best is yet to come! Your struggles are temporary! You are not home yet! A pain-free, tear-free, mourning-free, death-free life awaits you! How great is the Father's love . . . and his plan!

Enter his gates with thanksgiving and his courts with praise; give thanks to him and praise his name. (Psalm 100:4)

A LIFE OF THANKSGIVING

Prior to cancer, I lived a very ungrateful life. For years, I had taken for granted most of the things that God had blessed me with . . . including life itself! Cancer changed all that, though, and I began to live a life of thanksgiving. Besides learning to thank God back then, I also learned to give thanks to God, no matter what my situation is. Giving thanks during hard times doesn't come naturally, but with God's help, we can choose to be thankful no matter what! Throughout the Bible we are called to give thanks to God; and Psalm 118:1 gives us some reasons why: "Give thanks to the Lord, for he is good; his love endures forever." How about you? What can you thank God for today? Even during hard times, there is much to be thankful for. "Enter his gates with thanksgiving and his courts with praise; give thanks to him and praise his name." Today could be the start of a whole new way of life for you—a life of thanksgiving—a very good way to live! Thank you, God, for . . .

May the God of hope fill you with all joy and peace as you trust in him, so that you may overflow with hope by the power of the Holy Spirit.

(Romans 15:13)

GUARD YOUR JOY!

Joy is one of the greatest gifts available to believers in Jesus. And what is biblical joy? Biblical joy is a God-given rejoicing of the heart. Unlike happiness, joy is not dependent upon our circumstances. I have known great joy in my life ... even years ago within the crucible of cancer. While on the cancer journey, though, I discovered that my enemy, Satan, was always trying to steal my joy! I determined back then not to let him! Why would the enemy want to steal our joy? Because, as Nehemiah 8:10 tells us, "the joy of the LORD is your strength." If you're in need of some heavenly joy today, be on the lookout for joy-stealers in your life such as worry, unforgiveness or unbelief. Then be encouraged to know that, for every joy-stealer you may find in your life, there are joy-maintainers. For example, instead of worrying, we can maintain joy by *praying*. Instead of living with unforgiveness we can maintain joy by *forgiving* (with God's help). Or instead of unbelief . . . we can maintain joy by *trusting* God. Determine today not to let the enemy steal your joy! The joy of the Lord is your strength! Your strength! "May the God of hope fill you with all joy and peace as you trust in him, so that you may overflow with hope by the power of the Holy Spirit."

This is the day the LORD has made;

let us rejoice and be glad in it.

(Psalm 118:24, HCSB)

CHOOSING TO REJOICE

Whenever I read this verse or hear it quoted, I'm reminded of a story from years ago. Our son was in kindergarten, and his bus stop was a short walk from our front door. Rain or shine, while we waited for his bus to arrive, we sang a simple song based on Psalm 118:24. (In case you're wondering, he and I were the only ones at the bus stop when we sang!) At the time, I was still recovering from the more-than-harsh chemotherapy treatments I had undergone for stage-four ovarian cancer. I found that singing this little song always lifted my spirits, and it was a great way to start each day! I also discovered back then that I could choose to rejoice no matter what my circumstances were . . . what a valuable life lesson! This day, let's choose to rejoice and be glad in it. Why? Because this is the day the Lord has made . . . a gift from his hand to us.

The steadfast love of the LORD never ceases,

his mercies never come to an end;

they are new every morning;

great is your faithfulness.

(Lamentations 3:22–23, NRSV)

NEED HOPE?

Jeremiah, the author of Lamentations, explained in verse 21 of chapter 3 that bringing these words to mind gave him hope: "The steadfast love of the LORD never ceases, his mercies never come to an end; they are new every morning; great is your faithfulness." Those same words have also given me hope many times when I've brought them to mind. They remind me that no matter how difficult things get, I can always know that God's love for me won't cease, that God's mercies are new every morning and that God is always faithful. What encouraging, hope-filled truths! I once heard a pastor on the radio describe mercy as "divine compassion in action." That phrase really stuck with me. Read today's verses again; and when you come to the word *mercies*, think *divine compassion in action*. In action. God is never a passive and uninvolved heavenly Father, but rather the one who works on behalf of his children . . . taking action. If you're in need of hope, I encourage you to ponder Lamentations 3:22–23. And watch hope soar . . . hope soar!

The LORD is good,

a refuge in times of trouble.

(Nahum 1:7)

LIFE IS HARD, BUT GOD IS . . .

The Bible tells us that the Lord is good (see Psalm 25:8, Psalm 34:8, Psalm 118:1 and Nahum 1:7 above), and it's easy to believe this when life is going well! But when life is difficult, will we continue to believe that God is good? During my third cancer journey, within a span of seven months, here's a sampling of what my family and I experienced: cancer diagnoses for both my dad and me, many doctor visits for each of us, as well as major surgery for me and hospitalizations for us both, a move for my dad, the sale of my childhood home and, sadly, the death of my dad. Though life was hard back then, I continued to believe that God is good . . . choosing to believe God's Word over my circumstances. By believing that God is good, I was enabled to trust God in that valley, which brought peace to my heart. During hard times, our enemy Satan may try to convince us that God is not good (the same lie he used with Eve in the Garden of Eden), but this clearly contradicts what God's Word tells us! According to the Bible, God is good. His very nature is good. We see his goodness revealed time and again through the stories of the Bible as well as in the stories of our own lives. The Bible tells us that, in addition to being good, God is also compassionate and gracious, slow to anger and abounding in love and faithfulness (Psalm 86:15). When you think of God, is this how you picture him? If not, I encourage you to pick up the Bible and discover for yourself who God really is. Knowing who God is makes all the difference in our lives during the good times as well as during the challenging times. When you're being crushed by difficult times, I encourage you to begin to believe—or continue to believe—that God is good. Don't believe Satan's lie that he isn't! Remember . . . even though God is good, it doesn't mean bad things won't happen . . . for we live in a sin-stained world. Yes, life is hard, but God is good, "and we know that in all things God works for the good of those who love him, who have been called according to his purpose" (Romans 8:28). *Thank you, Lord, that you are good and working for the good of your children . . . no matter what circumstances surround us.*

"We do not know what to do,
but our eyes are on you."
(2 Chronicles 20:12)

A SIMPLE PRAYER

In 2 Chronicles 20, we're told that when a vast army was coming to make war on King Jehoshaphat, he sought God and proclaimed a fast for all of Judah. The people of Judah also began to seek help from the Lord, and during that time Jehoshaphat prayed in the midst of the people. Verse 12 of this chapter records the king's prayer: "We do not know what to do, but our eyes are on you." When troubles come into my life or into the lives of those I love, I often pray those same words. For years my pride convinced me that I could handle things on my own and didn't need to depend on anyone . . . not even God! Thankfully, God taught me that he wants me to depend on him! When troubling circumstances are surrounding you, try praying the words of King Jehoshaphat: *"We do not know what to do, but our eyes are on you."* Through those words, you will reveal your dependence on God, which is exactly how he wants you and me to live . . . today and every day!

All I need to do is cry to him—oh, praise the Lord—and I am saved from all my enemies!

(Psalm 18:3, TLB)

SAVED FROM MY ENEMIES

On my third cancer journey, I began to recognize fear, doubt and self-pity as real enemies in my life. During that time, God used Psalm 18:3 to teach me that, when I call on him, he comes and saves me from my enemies. After learning that truth, I began to apply it in my life. For example, when my enemy of fear attacked, I would immediately begin to call out to Jesus, just as the Psalm instructed me. Sometimes I called out verbally, other times I called out in silent prayer, "Jesus, help!" And Jesus never let me down. He always came. He always saved me from my enemies. Can you recognize an enemy at work in your life today? An enemy such as fear or doubt or self-pity? If so, then call on Jesus. He is able to save you from your enemies! He is the King of kings and Lord of lords! And mighty in battle is he! "All I need to do is cry to him—oh, praise the Lord—and I am saved from all my enemies!"

Whatever a man sows,

this he will also reap.

(Galatians 6:7, NASB)

A NEGATIVE ATTITUDE?

Are you being held captive by a negative attitude? Years ago I was, but I'll never forget the day this all changed! Back then a friend suggested that I listen to a certain radio pastor, so one morning I tuned in to his program. In his sermon that particular day, the pastor mentioned the fact that we have control over our own attitudes. As soon as those words fell from his lips, they stayed with me; and I soon recognized that I had daily been letting my circumstances determine my attitude. Relief flooded my heart as I realized I was in control of my attitude and didn't have to live another day imprisoned by a negative one. From that day forward, I determined to daily choose a positive attitude instead of the negative one I had been lugging around. Amazingly, as I became more positive, the people around me did, too. If you find yourself imprisoned by a crummy attitude, know that you don't have to live like that any longer . . . the choice is up to you! Like me, you have control over your own attitude. I am forever thankful I tuned in to that radio pastor's show that day, for the fact I gleaned from him was life-changing. I was set free! What attitudes have you been carrying around lately? Is it time for a change? You have control over your own attitude, just as I have over mine . . . daily! "Whatever a man sows, this he will also reap."

"So don't be anxious about tomorrow.

God will take care of your tomorrow too.

Live one day at a time."

(Matthew 6:34, TLB)

ONE DAY AT A TIME

While growing up, I often heard this statement: "Live one day at a time." Years later, when fears threatened to consume me during hard times, my dad spoke those familiar words to me again. Thankfully, I heeded his advice and began living just one day at a time. How did I do that? By praying and trusting that God would take care of me no matter what. I also began refusing to let fears about tomorrow steal the gift of each new day. Eventually, I came across the same words my dad had spoken to me—in the Bible . . . his advice to me had been biblical! My earthly father knew, and my heavenly Father knows, that living one day at a time is the best way to live. I'm so glad they shared it with me! Are you anxious about tomorrow? Like me, try living one day at a time. Refuse to let fears about tomorrow steal the gift of today. Instead, pray and trust that God will take care of you no matter what because he is faithful and takes care of his own. We have his word on it, and he cannot lie! "So don't be anxious about tomorrow. God will take care of your tomorrow too. Live one day at a time."

"We must go through many hardships to enter the kingdom of God," they said. (Acts 14:22)

NOT HOME YET

These words were originally spoken to the early church to encourage the disciples to remain true to the faith. Reading the same words years ago, I was encouraged to persevere in my faith, just as those early followers of Christ Jesus were. As believers, we are never promised a struggle-free life. Rather, we are clearly told in the Bible that we *will* suffer . . . this side of heaven. The good news is that one day our suffering will end forever (see Revelation 21:4); and in the meantime, we as believers in Jesus can experience God's peace and joy, even amidst our suffering. Times of suffering are an opportunity to come to know God better (who he is and what he can do) as we trust him with our suffering and seek him through prayer and reading the Bible. If you are a suffering child of God, I want you to know that the best is yet to come, and that, according to Romans 8:37, "we are *more than conquerors.*" Even so, "we must go through many hardships to enter the kingdom of God." We aren't home yet. We aren't home yet.

Have mercy on me, Lord,

for I call to you all day long.

(Psalm 86:3)

GOD'S MERCY

Years ago I heard God's mercy described as "divine compassion in action." Looking back, I clearly recognize God's mercy at work in my life. For example, it was his mercy that rescued me from myself and from the path of self-destruction that I had followed for several years before cancer struck. God's mercy also relieved me of self-pity and hopelessness and kept me from living in anger and bitterness through four cancer diagnoses. I am forever thankful for God's mercy in my life! Years ago God inspired me to write a song about mercy based on a Bible study I was facilitating at that time. Here are some of the lyrics from that song: *Lord, let your mercy wash over me, more than your blessing it's mercy I need. When I do not understand, Lord, your methods or your plan, let your mercy wash over me. When I'm blinded by my fears and my eyes are full of tears, let your mercy wash over me.* Are you in need of God's mercy? If so, may the psalmists' words become the cry of your heart today: "Let Your tender mercies come speedily to meet us, for we have been brought very low" (Psalm 79:8, NKJV); and "Have mercy on me, Lord, for I call to you all day long" (Psalm 86:3). God is a God of mercy; and, according to Psalm 136:1, "His mercy endures forever" (NKJV). Cry out for God's mercy today.

"And his name shall be the hope of all the world."

(Matthew 12:21, TLB)

HOPE HAS A NAME

In October of 1991, I was without God and without hope. At the time, I was thirty-three years old and had just been diagnosed with stage-four ovarian cancer. From that pit of despair, I began seeking God through prayer and reading a Bible that a friend had given me. Little by little I came to know the truth about God and his Son, Jesus Christ. Face to face with death, I eventually realized my need for a Savior, repented of my sins, and trusted in Jesus as Savior and Lord. With Jesus in my life, hope sprang up within me. A renowned surgeon once said, "A man can live three weeks without food, three days without water, and three minutes without air, but he cannot live three seconds without hope." Indeed, hope has been an essential part of my survival story . . . the kind of hope that comes through a relationship with Jesus. It's the kind of hope that 1 Peter 1:3 calls "living"—living because Jesus rose from the dead and offers us the hope of eternal life. It's also the kind of hope that the Bible says "will never disappoint us" (Romans 5:5, NCV), and is an "anchor for the soul" (Hebrews 6:19, NCV). How about you? Do you have the kind of hope that is available to all through Jesus? Or are you in need of hope? If you are feeling hopeless today instead of hopeful, I invite you not to give up . . . but to look up. Jesus waits with open arms. He's the one who died that you might live . . . the one in whom true hope is found. Yes, hope has a name: Jesus. "And his name shall be the hope of all the world."

Trust in him at all times, you people;

pour out your hearts to him,

for God is our refuge.

(Psalm 62:8)

BEING HONEST WITH GOD

I was newly diagnosed with cancer back in 1991 when someone gave me a copy of *Psalms Now*, a book of the Psalms in contemporary language. As I began to read the book, I was immediately drawn to it, for I saw my feelings mirrored in the psalmists' feelings as they honestly poured their hearts out to God. Through their honesty, I learned to be honest with God myself. Consider these words from the psalmists' hearts: "My tears have been my food day and night, while people say to me all day long, 'Where is your God?'" (Psalm 42:3); "Save me, O God, for the waters have come up to my neck. I sink in the miry depths, where there is no foothold. I have come into the deep waters; the floods engulf me" (Psalm 69:1–2); "Have mercy on me, my God, have mercy on me, for in you I take refuge. I will take refuge in the shadow of your wings until the disaster has passed" (Psalm 57:1). Throughout the Psalms, we see the writers pouring their hearts out to God. Why are we to pour out our hearts to the Lord? Psalm 62:8 tells us it's because "God is our refuge" (meaning shelter or place of protection). Choose to pour out your heart to God today. God can handle it! And thanks to the book of Psalms, I know this is true! "Trust in him at all times, you people; pour out your hearts to him, for God is our refuge."

Trust in the LORD with all your heart

and lean not on your own understanding.

(Proverbs 3:5)

TRUST AND LEAN NOT

When I come across this verse, I'm often reminded of my first cancer journey . . . a time when I was daily confronted with a choice: would I walk by faith, trusting God? Or would I lean on my own understanding and believe what my circumstances were dictating to me? To be honest, I looked as if I were on the brink of death back then. Never heavy in the first place, I had lost about forty pounds . . . my body ravaged by the chemotherapy. During that time, though, God clearly revealed to me through Scripture that he was going to heal me. Thankfully, I chose to trust God and not lean on my own understanding, which would have surely convinced me that I was soon headed for the grave . . . but this was a lie. Why should we trust God? Here are some verses to consider:

Psalm 84:12 - LORD Almighty, blessed is the one who trusts in you.

Psalm 28:7 - My heart trusts in him, and he helps me.

Psalm 32:10 - Many are the woes of the wicked, but the LORD's unfailing love surrounds the one who trusts in him.

Isaiah 26:3 - You will keep in perfect peace those whose minds are steadfast, because they trust in you.

Nahum 1:7 - The LORD is good, a refuge in times of trouble. He cares for those who trust in him.

Psalm 125:1 - Those who trust in the LORD are like Mount Zion, which cannot be shaken but endures forever.

As you can see, there are definitely benefits to trusting God! Scripture also teaches us that without faith it's impossible to please God, and as believers we want to please him! May you choose to *trust* and *lean not* today.

Summon your power, God;

show us your strength, our God,

as you have done before.

(Psalm 68:28)

PRAYING GOD'S WORD

The Bible tells us that God's Word is "powerful" (Hebrews 4:12, NKJV) and that the prayer of the righteous is "powerful and effective" (James 5:16). When we combine God's Word and prayer, we have a powerful and effective way to pray! Praying God's Word is praying the very words of God—his language—back to him. For example, when a difficult circumstance came up at my husband's workplace, I prayed Psalm 68:28, which says, "Summon your power, God; show us your strength, our God, as you have done before." Another time I prayed Psalm 61:7—"appoint your love and faithfulness to protect him"—for a friend's son who was traveling in Asia at the time: *Appoint your love and faithfulness to protect Andrew, Lord.* Years ago I daily prayed Psalm 107:14—"He brought them out of darkness and gloom and broke their chains apart" (HCSB)—for a friend experiencing depression amidst dark times: *Bring him out of darkness and gloom, Lord, and break his chains apart.* God has given us his Word, and it is a powerful weapon when we pray it amidst the battles of our lives. When you're reading the Bible and a passage seems to jump out at you, try turning it into a prayer. Praying God's Word is one way to pray . . . a powerful way . . . an effective way . . . try it today!

*"Then you will know the truth,
and the truth will set you free."
(John 8:32)*

TRUTH SETS US FREE!

Psalm 86:5 tells us that God is good; he is ready to forgive and he is abounding in lovingkindness to all who call on him. This is who the God of the Bible really is. Is this the God whom you know? For years, I had a wrong perception of who God really is—a perception based on what others had told me and what my own imagination had convinced me to believe about God. Then a friend gave me a Bible; and in the midst of difficult times, I began absorbing wisdom from its pages . . . soaking it all up like a sponge. Eventually, I came to know the truth about God, and I began replacing all the lies I had believed about him with the truth of God's Word. Jesus said this, "Then you will know the truth, and the truth will set you free." Knowing the truth about God truly has set me free . . . free from worry, fear, shame and guilt! Are you in need of some truth about God? If so, ponder Psalm 86:5 today. Then choose to read the Bible, where truth abounds about God, ourselves, others, life and so much more! The truth really does set us free. "For You, Lord, are good, and ready to forgive, and abundant in lovingkindness to all who call upon You" (NASB). How's that for starters?

And the God of all grace, who called you to his eternal glory in Christ, after you have suffered a little while, will himself restore you and make you strong, firm and steadfast.

(1 Peter 5:10)

CHOICES

I would like to encourage you today by sharing some of the things I choose to do during times of suffering in my own life. Look for the actions and attitudes in **boldface** in the Scriptures below. They are actions and attitudes that have helped me to live victoriously, even while surrounded by difficult trials; and they are taken straight from the Word of God.

Psalm 56:3 - When I am afraid, **I put my trust in you**.

1 Peter 5:8–9 - **Be alert and of sober mind**. Your enemy the devil prowls around like a roaring lion looking for someone to devour. **Resist him, standing firm in the faith**.

Acts 16:24–25 - When he received these orders, he put them in the inner cell and fastened their feet in the stocks. About midnight Paul and Silas were **praying and singing hymns to God**, and the other prisoners were listening to them.

Psalm 106:12 - Then they **believed his promises and sang his praise**.

Philippians 4:6, NLT - **Don't worry** about anything; **instead, pray** about everything.

1 Thessalonians 5:18 - **Give thanks in all circumstances**; for this is God's will for you in Christ Jesus.

Philippians 4:4 - **Rejoice in the Lord** always.

2 Chronicles 32:26 - Then Hezekiah **repented of the pride of his heart**.

2 Chronicles 20:12 - "We do not know what to do, but **our eyes are on you**."

Psalm 37:7 - **Be still before the LORD** and **wait patiently for him**.

Psalm 119:92, NKJV - Unless **Your law had been my delight**, I would then have perished in my affliction.

Lamentations 3:54–55, NKJV - The waters flowed over my head; I said, "I am cut off!" **I called on Your name**, O LORD, from the lowest pit.

Hebrews 12:1–2 - **Let us run with perseverance the race marked out for us, fixing our eyes on Jesus**, the pioneer and perfecter of faith.

Hebrews 12:3 - **Consider him** who endured such opposition from sinners, so that you will not grow weary and lose heart.

Matthew 26:39 - **"Yet not as I will, but as you will."**

Psalm 27:13, NKJV - I would have lost heart, unless I had **believed that I would see the goodness of the LORD in the land of the living**.

Don't let circumstances paralyze you from taking action. Which Scriptures spoke to you from the list above? Choose to incorporate them into your life today. And remember what 1 Peter 5:10 tells us: "And the God of all grace, who called you to his eternal glory in Christ, after you have suffered a little while, will himself restore you and make you strong, firm and steadfast." Hold on to that promise today in the midst of your own trials, which, according to this verse, are temporary . . . temporary! This is great news for children of God who are suffering.

*W*hen I am afraid, I will trust in You.

(Psalm 56:3, HCSB)

RESOLVE TO DO OR NOT TO DO

King Jehoshaphat, according to 2 Chronicles 20:3, "resolved to inquire of the Lord." Psalm 17:3 tells us that David determined, or resolved, that his mouth would not sin. And in Daniel 1:8 we're told that Daniel, who had been taken captive in Babylon, "resolved not to defile himself with the royal food and wine." The word *resolve* means to reach a firm decision about . . . to determine in one's heart . . . to make up one's mind . . . to be committed to a course of action. As a believer in Jesus, I have resolved to do and not to do certain things. For example, I resolved long ago to trust God, instead of worrying, when fear comes storming in. This is clearly what David had resolved to do too, as we read in Psalm 56:3, "When I am afraid, I will trust in You." If I hadn't resolved to trust God in the face of fear, I surely would have given into fear every single time on my cancer journey; and eventually I would have been held captive by it. So what about you? Are there things you have resolved to do or not to do in your life? If not, why not start today? I resolve to_____. Or I resolve not to_____. God can help you stand firm in your resolve to do and not do certain things. For years God has helped me to trust him—but only after I *resolved* to trust him—even when fear comes storming in. And I believe David would have said the same—right along with Daniel and Jehoshaphat.

"My ears had heard of you before,
but now my eyes have seen you."
(Job 42:5, NCV)

PERSONAL KNOWLEDGE OF GOD

Job's original knowledge of God came from what others had told him . . . what he had heard. Then, in the midst of great and heart-wrenching trials, Job came to a personal knowledge of God, a knowledge that enabled him to say, "but now my eyes have seen you." For much of my life, my knowledge of God also came from what I had heard from others. During a grueling and almost unbearable cancer experience in 1991, though, God began revealing himself to me personally as I sought him through prayer and reading the Bible. Eventually I, like Job, could say, "but now my eyes have seen you." None of us like hardship; but it's through hardship that God often reveals himself to us, and we see him more clearly. I have found that tears have a way of preparing the eyes for a magnificent view of him! Surrounded by hardship today, look for God. He is there! Your hardship is an opportunity to know God . . . instead of just knowing *about* him. Take it from Job, me and countless others . . . there's nothing like a personal knowledge of God. It's life changing. Life changing indeed! See for yourself.

God is our refuge and strength,

a very present help in trouble.

(Psalm 46:1, NKJV)

OUR REFUGE AND STRENGTH

In the aftermath of the horrific terrorist attacks of September 11, 2001, Psalm 46:1 came to my mind, "God is our refuge and strength, a very present help in trouble." While the horrible recorded events of that day played over and over again on the television screen and in my mind, Psalm 46:1 reminded me that God *is* my refuge, strength and very present help in trouble. God had helped me time and again before that day, and I knew that he would continue to help me . . . as well as our country. Psalm 46:1 also helped me back then to focus on God instead of focusing on the trouble at hand. Are you in need of refuge or strength today? Are you in need of a very present help? Know that God is all of that, and that he wants to be all of that for *you*. Will you ask God to be that in your life today? As his child, you can count on the fact that he is for you . . . not against you. The storms of life may rage; but refuge, strength and help are available. In him! In him!

You are my rock and my fortress;

for Your name's sake You will lead me and guide me.

(Psalm 31:3, NASB)

AN "ARE, HAVE AND WILL" PRAYER

Psalm 31 is one of King David's many psalms in which he poured out his heart to the Lord. While pondering that psalm one day, I was struck by three repeated words that stood out to me . . . ***are, have*** and ***will*** . . . words that David used while referring to the Lord. *Are* shows who God consistently is—these statements reveal his character. *Have* expresses what he has already accomplished, indicating that we can look back and be thankful for what he's done. *Will* shows what he promises to do, helping us know that we can trust him for the future. Check out for yourself the following verses from Psalm 31 that include these words in connection with the Lord:

Verse 3 - You **are** my rock and my fortress.

Verse 4 - For You **are** my strength.

Verse 14 - But as for me, I trust in You, O LORD, I say, "You **are** my God."

Verse 5 - You **have** ransomed me, O LORD, God of truth.

Verse 7 - I will rejoice and be glad in Your lovingkindness, because You **have** seen my affliction; You **have** known the troubles of my soul.

Verse 8 - And You have not given me over into the hand of the enemy; You **have** set my feet in a large place.

Verse 19 - How great is Your goodness, which You **have** stored up for those who fear You, which You **have** wrought for those who take refuge in You, before the sons of men!

Verse 3 - For Your name's sake You **will** lead me and guide me.

Verse 4 - You **will** pull me out of the net which they have secretly laid for me.

After reading Psalm 31 one morning, I happened to receive a call requesting my help with something . . . something that would normally have pushed me a little out of my comfort zone! As I prayed about that request, I incorporated those same three words that David used in Psalm 31.

I encourage you today to consider a difficult circumstance in your life; and as you pray about it, apply David's pattern from Psalm 31 (by declaring truths about who God is, how he has already worked in your life and how he will continue to work in your life). And if you do pray an "*are, have* and *will*" prayer today regarding a present circumstance in your life, I believe faith will arise. Faith will arise—just as it did for me!

"For my thoughts are not your thoughts,

neither are your ways my ways," declares the LORD.

"As the heavens are higher than the earth,

so are my ways higher than your ways

and my thoughts than your thoughts."

(Isaiah 55:8–9)

UNANSWERED "WHY?" QUESTIONS

It seems as if we all have unanswered "why?" questions for God. Those questions seem to surface most when the tragedies of life come knocking. There's a passage from the Old Testament that has often helped me in dealing with unanswered "why?" questions: "'For my thoughts are not your thoughts, neither are your ways my ways,' declares the LORD. 'As the heavens are higher than the earth, so are my ways higher than your ways and my thoughts than your thoughts.'" Those verses remind me that God is not altogether like me. God is God, and I am not. These verses also remind me that God's thoughts and ways are not my thoughts and ways and that he is so much bigger than I can even imagine! God is good, loving, forgiving, faithful, perfect, all-knowing, merciful, all-powerful and so much more. And God invites me . . . all of me—including my unanswered "why?" questions—to rest in the knowledge of who he is. There are some questions that just won't be answered this side of heaven. Choose today to give up the struggle with any unanswered questions; and snuggle instead . . . resting in the Father's arms and in the truth of who he is.

But they that wait upon the LORD shall renew their strength; they shall mount up with wings as eagles; they shall run, and not be weary; and they shall walk, and not faint.

(Isaiah 40:31, KJV)

WAITING ON THE LORD

One morning some song lyrics played in my mind, lyrics that tell about how strength will rise as we wait on the Lord. For the first time ever, I realized those lyrics were most likely based on Isaiah 40:31. According to the *Hebrew-Greek Key Word Study Bible*, the original Hebrew word for *wait upon*, which is used in this verse, is "a verb meaning to wait for, to look for, to hope for." Waiting on the Lord is not passive. Rather it involves confident expectation and hope! Years ago, when I was so very physically weak with cancer, I sensed God personally speaking to me through Isaiah 40:31, promising me renewed strength and more if I waited on him. I immediately began waiting on God, and he was true to his promise . . . my strength was renewed (not overnight, but eventually). Are you in need of strength? Maybe it's time to quit striving, and instead wait on the Lord as I finally did, trusting on him to come through as I meditated on that verse: "But they that wait upon the LORD shall renew their strength; they shall mount up with wings as eagles; they shall run, and not be weary; and they shall walk, and not faint." Strength comes from the Lord, and Isaiah 40:31 encourages us to wait on him when we are in need of strength.

He heals the brokenhearted

and binds up their wounds.

(Psalm 147:3)

JESUS AND THE BROKENHEARTED

It seems as if we live in a world full of broken hearts . . . hearts that have been broken through physical and verbal abuse, rejection, loss of all kinds, betrayal and more. Years ago I experienced a broken heart myself after saying goodbye to my dear friend Deb, who moved far away to Oregon from Minnesota, where I live. Thinking about broken hearts, I'm reminded of this verse: "He heals the brokenhearted and binds up their wounds," along with this one: "The LORD is close to the brokenhearted and saves those who are crushed in spirit" (Psalm 34:18). I'm also reminded of this prophecy written about Jesus hundreds of years before his birth: "He has sent me to bind up the brokenhearted" (Isaiah 61:1). The original Hebrew word for *bind up*, which is used in this verse, is *chabash*. According to the *Hebrew-Greek Key Word Study Bible*, "this word is often used to describe binding wounds (both physical and spiritual) with the result that healing occurs." Are you struggling with a broken heart today? If so, call on Jesus. Call on Jesus. The One who, according to the previous verses, heals the brokenhearted, is close to the brokenhearted and binds up the brokenhearted . . . with bandages of mercy, grace, love and forgiveness. Jesus personally knows what it's like to have a broken heart. Just think of all he endured this side of heaven. And know this: Jesus can even mend those hearts that seem beyond repair. He's done it for me. He can do it for you. Trust him with your broken heart today, and know that healing is on the way! "He heals the brokenhearted and binds up their wounds."

"*Father, if you are willing, take this cup from me;*

yet not my will, but yours be done."

(Luke 22:42)

SUBMITTING TO GOD'S WILL

After struggling in the garden of Gethsemane over his Father's will for him—the cross—Jesus uttered these humble and submissive words: "yet not my will, but yours be done." Jesus shared his heart with his Father, asking for—if God was willing—the cup of suffering that lay ahead of him to be taken away. In the end, amidst terrible anguish and sweat like drops of blood (Luke 22:44), Jesus submitted to his Father's will. During my second cancer I, too, chose to submit to God's will . . . accept my circumstances. And that choice enabled me to move on and ask, "What now?" instead of getting stuck in anger and bitterness, a dead-end street I never want to live on. When we submit to God's will during hard times, we are saying to God, "I trust you." Submission is a sign of humility and faith. Lack of submission often stems from pride or unbelief. Submitting to God's will during hard times may be the hardest thing we are ever called on to do. Yet consider all that was accomplished through Jesus' submission . . . forgiveness of sins, eternal life, peace with God and victory over sin and death! Know that God will accomplish great things when *you* choose to submit to him . . . especially during hard times. When you, like Jesus, say, "Not my will, but yours be done."

He got up, rebuked the wind and said to the waves,

"Quiet! Be still!"

Then the wind died down and

it was completely calm.

(Mark 4:39)

GOD'S PERSPECTIVE

One morning I woke up with a certain situation on my mind, and I thought to myself, *I need to ask God for a word regarding it, to get his perspective on it.* With that thought on my mind, I was reminded of a story from the pages of the Bible. One night Jesus was with his disciples in a boat when a storm arose . . . a big storm! The Bible describes it like this: "A furious squall came up, and the waves broke over the boat, so that it was nearly swamped" (Mark 4:37). Jesus slept through the storm while his disciples panicked. They assumed they were going to drown. But they were looking at their situation from their own limited perspective . . . not from God's. When the disciples woke Jesus up, "He got up, rebuked the wind and said to the waves, 'Quiet! Be still!' Then the wind died down and it was completely calm." What hard situation are you dealing with in your life today? What kind of storm is raging? Don't let yourself be consumed by your own thoughts regarding it. Instead, ask God for his perspective, knowing that God's point of view may be completely opposite of what you're thinking. You may think you're drowning, but God could be setting things up for a miracle. And remember this . . . when he speaks, the storms of life must bow to his authority! He is in control . . . in control! Even when it seems as if he's sleeping . . .

"Far be it from you to do such a thing—

to kill the righteous with the wicked,

treating the righteous and the wicked alike.

Far be it from you!

Will not the Judge of all the earth do right?"

(Genesis 18:25)

PRAYERS BASED ON TRUTH

I remember when our pastor spoke on Nehemiah's prayer, found in Nehemiah 1:5–11. After learning truths found in that prayer, I decided to start reading some of the other prayers found in the Bible. Soon afterward, in the back of my Bible, I found references for many of those prayers. The first prayer listed was one of Abraham's prayers found in Genesis 18:22–33. In that prayer, Abraham is pleading to God on behalf of the wicked city of Sodom. In Genesis 18:25, Abraham says to God, "Far be it from you to do such a thing—to kill the righteous with the wicked, treating the righteous and the wicked alike. Far be it from you! Will not the Judge of all the earth do right?" Pondering those words, I realized that Abraham's requests were based on who he knew God was . . . the judge (or ruler) of all the earth who *does* do what is right. When I had stage-four ovarian cancer, my prayers were also based on who I knew God was. For example, I had read in the Bible that "nothing is impossible for God" (Luke 1:37, GW). I believed those words back then and began basing my prayers on that truth. I was in an impossible situation, but since "nothing is impossible for God," I asked for what many considered impossible . . . healing from stage-four ovarian cancer. As you consider your own prayers, are they based on the truth of who God is according to God's Word? If not, be like Abraham and countless others, and learn to base your prayer requests on who God really is—loving, kind, forgiving, merciful, all-powerful, all-knowing and compassionate. Knowing who God really is should turn our prayers into big prayers! Big prayers for a big God!

You, LORD, *hear the desire of the afflicted;*
you encourage them, and you listen to their cry.
(Psalm 10:17)

GOD ENCOURAGES

What a tender portrait of God is painted for us through the words of Psalm 10:17. Within the crucible of affliction, how comforting it is to know that God hears our desires and listens to our cries. Thinking on that, I'm reminded of Psalm 56:8. The words of the New Living Translation describe it so well—"You keep track of all my sorrows. You have collected all my tears in your bottle. You have recorded each one in your book." Even when no one else seems to care, we can know for certain that God does! Psalm 10:17 also tells us that God encourages the afflicted. The God of the Bible is the God who encourages! At times he encourages us through the pages of the Bible. In other times, he may use other people to lift us up, which reminds me of my dear friend Barb. God mightily used her in my life, especially to encourage me during my first cancer journey. Every single time I was in need of extra reassurance back then, I would find a card in our mailbox from Barb. It was God who knew when I was in need of additional encouragement, and he provided that encouragement many times through Barb! Are you afflicted? Do you need to be lifted up? If so, then know that the God of the Bible is the God who encourages, who hears your desire, listens to your cry, keeps track of all your sorrows, collects your tears in his bottle and records each one in his book. May the God who encourages, encourage *you* today!

The LORD is in his holy temple;

the LORD is on his heavenly throne.

(Psalm 11:4)

JESUS IS ON THE THRONE

One night, when reading this verse, I was reminded of an incident in my life. At the hospital, the day before surgery for my third cancer, I ran into a nurse I knew named Bonnie. After learning of my cancer and scheduled surgery, the first words out of Bonnie's mouth were, "Jesus is on the throne." I didn't consider those words to be especially important at first, and I didn't consider their significance until I pondered them later that night; and then . . . how they comforted and encouraged me! It was then that I realized anew that Jesus truly *is* on the throne. He was in control at that moment. In control of my situation, the surgery, the cancer, my doctors . . . everything! May Bonnie's words to me so long ago comfort and encourage you today! Jesus *is* still on the throne. And when, as children of God, we feel that truth move from our heads to our hearts, a settled peace and an unshakeable hope rise up within us! Yes, Jesus is King! He is on the throne. Mighty and victorious is he!

In all this you greatly rejoice, though now for a little while you may have had to suffer grief in all kinds of trials. These have come so that the proven genuineness of your faith—of greater worth than gold, which perishes even though refined by fire—may result in praise, glory and honor when Jesus Christ is revealed.

(1 Peter 1:6–7)

GENUINE FAITH?

Have you ever considered that your trials have come to reveal the genuineness of your faith? In 1 Peter 1:6–7, the Bible tells us this is true. When life is going well, it's easy to say that we trust God. But let the trials come, and then we find out where we really stand. I have seen people profess strong faith until a trial hit . . . then that faith was nowhere to be found! What is your current trial revealing about your faith—to God, to others, and even to yourself? Is your faith a genuine faith? Strong enough to stand up under trial? Is it one that believes God . . . no matter what? Or is your trial revealing no evidence of faith at all? (Know that you can ask God for faith!) God allows trials into our lives for our good and his glory. How it must bless his heart to see a genuine faith rise to the surface during a difficult trial in the life of one of his children! When trials come—and they will—think of them as faith tests. And may you pass those tests, trusting God even when you don't understand.

As you know, it was because of an illness

that I first preached the gospel to you.

(Galatians 4:13)

USING SUFFERING FOR GOD'S PURPOSES

My four-time cancer journey was full of opportunities to testify to God's love, faithfulness, strength, peace, joy, his Son Jesus Christ and his deeds on my behalf. Looking back on my journey, I recall sharing about God with family, friends, hospital staff and patients. I shared in doctors' offices, during medical exams, in waiting rooms and wherever else I had an opportunity to share! In Galatians 4:13, Paul wrote that it was because of an illness he had first preached the gospel to the Galatians. Could it be that God has allowed *your* illness or trial so that others may hear of him? Or hear the gospel, believe and live? As you deal with an illness or another kind of trial today, may God open your eyes to see his purposes within it . . . purposes that may mean hope or even eternal life for someone else. "As you know, it was because of an illness that I first preached the gospel to you." Don't waste your suffering. Rather use it for God's purposes today!

Then they cried out to the LORD in their trouble;

He delivered them out of their distresses.

(Psalm 107:6, NASB)

CRYING OUT TO THE LORD

In Psalm 107:1–32, we find four groups of people who are in distress. The first group is composed of wanderers. They are unsettled, not finding their way, hungry and thirsty with their lives ebbing away. The second group is made up of people who are enslaved, depressed and in great despair . . . with no one to help them. Why are they enslaved? Verse 11 states that it is "because they had rebelled against the words of God and spurned the counsel of the Most High" (NASB). The third group is composed of those who are afflicted. They have no appetite and are face to face with death. Why? Verse 17 tells us that these "fools, because of their rebellious way, and because of their iniquities, were afflicted" (NASB). The fourth and final distressed group includes those in the midst of a great storm. They are fearful and at their wits' end. Although the circumstances of the four groups of people varied, each group did the same thing when they were in distress. "They cried out to the Lord." And how did the Lord respond to them? We're told he delivered them, he saved them out of their distress. Every time I read Psalm 107, I'm amazed at how closely my past mirrors the third group of distressed people. How about you? Are you in distress today? Can you relate to any of the circumstances mentioned above? If so, then cry out to the Lord. He is merciful to those in distress, and he is all-powerful, too . . . able to deliver. That I know!

"This is an easy thing in the eyes of the LORD."

(2 Kings 3:18)

EASY IN THE EYES OF THE LORD

Tucked within the pages of 2 Kings, we find an interesting story. After Ahab (the King of Israel) died, the King of Moab rebelled against Joram (the new King of Israel). In response, Joram asked the King of Judah to join him in battle, and he agreed. The King of Edom also joined forces with them. After marching for seven days and reaching a valley, their army ran out of water for their animals and themselves. In trouble, the three kings went to see the prophet Elisha, whom they knew to be a mighty man of God. The Lord spoke through Elisha, telling the kings that, although they wouldn't see any wind or rain, the valley would be filled with water for them and their animals to drink! In verse 18, we read that "this is an easy thing in the eyes of the LORD." Then in verse 20, we're told that the next morning the land was filled with water! After pondering that remarkable story, I'm reminded anew to always look at things from God's perspective! What may look overwhelming and impossible from my point of view is an "easy thing in the eyes of the LORD." What is the most difficult circumstance in your life right now? Choose to look at it today from God's perspective. My_____(your difficult circumstance) "is an easy thing in the eyes of the LORD." Great and powerful is he!

If your law had not been my delight,
I would have perished in my affliction.
(Psalm 119:92)

DELIGHTING IN GOD'S WORD

God's Word—the Bible—is my delight, and it first became my delight back in 1992, during my intensive chemotherapy for ovarian cancer. Shortly after my diagnosis, as I mentioned earlier, a friend gave me a Bible. Weeks later, at Christmas, my husband gave me another Bible . . . a beautiful leather-bound copy that included insights on each page regarding how to apply God's Word to my daily life. That Bible became my constant companion. It wasn't too long afterwards, due to repeated use, that it looked as though it had been through a war! God's Word daily helped me to navigate and rise above the stormy seas of cancer back then. That Bible became stuffed full of notes and bookmarks, each of which I placed in there after discovering a new insight. One day a friend called and asked what I was doing. "Cleaning out my Bible," was my reply. My friend, who called me by my nickname laughed and said, "T, most people clean out their cupboards!" I haven't used that particular Bible in years, but whenever I spot it in my closet, its cracked edges and loose binding still remind me of the time when God's Word became my delight! I can easily relate to the psalmist's words in Psalm 119:92, "If your law had not been my delight, I would have perished in my affliction." Yes, without God's Word I, too, would have perished in my affliction . . . from despair, self-pity, fear and loneliness. In God's Word, I discovered God himself, and he has used his Word time and again to bring hope, strength, peace, conviction, correction and encouragement. "If your law had not been my delight, I would have perished in my affliction." Do you delight in God's Word? If not, ask him to help you to delight in it today.

"No matter what your situation is, there is always someone who is worse off than you are."

AN EARTHLY PERSPECTIVE

Years ago my husband, Pete, said to me, "No matter what your situation is, there is always someone who is worse off than you are." At the time, I was at the hospital waiting to undergo a procedure and immersed in self-pity. Back then I was literally skin and bones, weighing in at 90 pounds. With my white count under 1.0, I was so very sick. As I waited for my name to be called that day, a patient was wheeled past me in a wheelchair. It was the first person I had seen who actually looked sicker than I did. Drowning in hospital attire, sunk down in the wheelchair and wearing a facemask to protect him from germs, that patient looked as if he were on the brink of death. I was shocked at his appearance, and it was just then that Pete uttered those unforgettable words, "No matter what your situation is, there is always someone who is worse off than you are." Upon hearing that blunt statement, my perspective changed, and self-pity was sent packing. I immediately realized that my situation could have been even worse than it was; and that because I wasn't as sick as the other patient, I had much to be thankful for . . . even though significant troubles still surrounded me. I have never forgotten Pete's words to me back then—or the image of that gravely sick man. Although I strive to keep a heavenly perspective daily, there are times when an earthly perspective is just what I need . . . as I did that day at the hospital so long ago.

"Simon, Simon, behold, Satan demanded to have you, that he might sift you like wheat, but I have prayed for you that your faith may not fail."

(Luke 22:31–32, ESV)

UNFAILING FAITH

At the Last Supper, before heading to the cross, Jesus spoke to his disciple Simon Peter, "Simon, Simon, behold, Satan demanded to have you, that he might sift you like wheat, but I have prayed for you that your faith may not fail." After hearing those words, Peter told Jesus that he was ready to go with him to prison—and even to death. But Jesus replied that Peter would deny knowing him three times, and that very night Jesus' words were fulfilled. Satan came to sift Peter, and Peter denied his Lord. When Jesus told Peter that he had prayed for him, what was the prayer? That Simon Peter's faith would not fail. Later we find evidence that his faith did not fail when, after Jesus' death and resurrection, Peter became a strong leader of the early church. But I wonder . . . what if Jesus hadn't prayed for his disciple and friend? Might his faith have failed? Thinking of faith *not* failing, I'm reminded of the time John the Baptist was stuck in prison. After hearing about all the miracles of Jesus, John began wondering why Jesus hadn't rescued him from prison. Doubts began to swirl in his mind. What was Jesus' message to John in prison? "God blesses those who do not fall away because of me." (Luke 7:23, NLT). In other words, blessed is the man whose faith does not fail. I remember asking friends to pray that my faith would not fail during my first cancer. Although times were more than difficult, my faith did not fail! I encourage you to think of someone today who is going through a time of sifting . . . someone for whom you can pray for strong, unfailing faith. And if that someone is you, know that I have been praying and will continue to pray for everyone who will ever read this—including you—that your faith will never fail. I'm so thankful others prayed that for me!

He saw the disciples straining at the oars, because the wind was against them. Shortly before dawn he went out to them, walking on the lake.

(Mark 6:48)

JESUS SEES US IN THE STORM

Right after one of the loaves and fishes miracles, which fed a large and hungry crowd, Jesus made his disciples get into a boat to go on ahead of him to another place. A storm arose that night; and Jesus, who had stayed behind to pray, saw his disciples out on the lake . . . straining at the oars. After seeing his disciples struggling in the storm, Jesus went out to them. How? By walking on the water! When Jesus' disciples saw him walking on the water, they were terrified because they thought he was a ghost. Jesus told them it was he, to take courage and not to be afraid. Then he got in the boat with them, and the wind immediately died down. When I pondered that story, these insights came to mind:

> Jesus saw the disciples in the storm and knew exactly what was happening to them.
>
> In the storm, Jesus went to the disciples.
>
> Initially, the disciples did not recognize Jesus.
>
> During the storm, Jesus revealed himself in new ways to the disciples through the miraculous.

What applications can we draw from this story? In the storms of life, Jesus sees us and knows exactly what is happening to us. In the storms of life, Jesus comes to us. In the storms of life, we may not initially recognize Jesus' presence with us. And in the storms of life, Jesus may reveal himself to us in new ways, which may include the miraculous. Are you looking for Jesus in the storms of life? He is there. He is there. Keep your eyes on him . . . not on the storm.

But I trust in your unfailing love;

my heart rejoices in your salvation.

I will sing the LORD's praise,

for he has been good to me.

(Psalm 13:5–6)

TRUST, REJOICE AND SING

David, the mighty king and sweet psalmist of the Old Testament, wrote many of the psalms. After reading one of them, I couldn't help but notice the number of times he asked, "*How long?*" David begins Psalm 13 with that question and from there goes on to get more specific. "Will you forget me forever? *How long* will you hide your face from me?" (verse 1); "*How long* must I wrestle with my thoughts and day after day have sorrow in my heart? *How long* will my enemy triumph over me?" (verse 2). After that series of questions, David asks the Lord to look on him, answer him and give light to his eyes . . . without this, David believed he would sleep in death, which would give his enemies a reason to boast and rejoice. Then, in the last two verses of Psalm 13, we see David choosing to trust, rejoice and sing . . . and even though his "*How long?*" questions remained, David's words reveal his trust. "But I trust in your unfailing love; my heart rejoices in your salvation. I will sing the LORD's praise, for he has been good to me" (verses 5–6). Like me, do you have any "*How long?*" questions of your own? If so, will you, too, choose to trust in God's unfailing love, rejoice in his salvation and sing praise for his goodness? This could be your opportunity to shine for God (by trusting, rejoicing and singing) amidst difficulties and questions . . . a witness that God may one day use in drawing others to Jesus! Don't miss the opportunity! Don't miss it! Trust, rejoice and sing . . . today and every day, regardless of how long your "*How long?*" questions remain . . . regardless of how you feel. God is faithful . . . forever faithful . . . and the best is yet to come!

Surely it was for my benefit

that I suffered such anguish.

(Isaiah 38:17)

SUFFERING AND BENEFITS

Hezekiah, the king of Judah, became ill and was at the point of death when the prophet Isaiah arrived with a message from the Lord. What was that message? Hezekiah was to put his house in order because he was going to die. As the truth of that message sank in, Hezekiah, through tears, asked the Lord to remember his faithfulness and devotion to him. Following Hezekiah's prayer, Isaiah returned to him with another message from the Lord. Hezekiah was told that the Lord would add fifteen years to his life as well as deliver him and his city from the king of Assyria's hand. And to prove that he would do what he had said he would do, the Lord gave Hezekiah a miraculous sign. As always, the Lord was faithful to his promise, and Hezekiah recovered. After his illness and recovery, Hezekiah recorded the words found in Isaiah 38:17: "Surely it was for my benefit that I suffered such anguish." In verse 15 we discover one facet of that benefit: "I will walk humbly all my years because of this anguish of my soul." Looking back, Hezekiah recognized that he had suffered such anguish for his own good. This reminds me of Romans 8:28: "And we know that in all things God works for the good of those who love him, who have been called according to his purpose." Years ago, I came to believe

Romans 8:28, and I trusted that God was working for my good amidst the cancer journey. And looking back now, I know that "it was for my benefit that I suffered such anguish." What were some of the benefits God wrought in my life through suffering? I was humbled. I came to know God and his Son, Jesus. I learned to pray about everything. I learned to praise God in the good times and in the hard. I also learned to walk by faith, trusting God no matter what my circumstances were shouting at me. I eventually came to know that nothing is impossible with God! If you are a child of God, try looking at any suffering in your life with a "Hezekiah" or "Romans 8:28" perspective . . . knowing there will be benefits for you as you trust God each step of the way.

The angel of the LORD came back a second time and touched him and said, "Get up and eat, for the journey is too much for you."

(1 Kings 19:7)

WHEN THE JOURNEY IS TOO MUCH

The Old Testament prophet Elijah was afraid and running for his life. He had just defeated the prophets of Baal on Mount Carmel, and wicked Jezebel wanted him dead. After arriving in Beersheba, Elijah left his servant there and journeyed solo into the desert. Sitting under a broom tree, he prayed that he would die. He had had enough . . . maybe you can relate. After praying and falling asleep under the tree, Elijah was touched by the angel of the Lord, who told him to get up and eat. Looking around, Elijah discovered heavenly provision right there in the desert . . . baked bread and a jar of water. He ate and drank and lay down again. In 1 Kings 19:7, we learn what happened next. "The angel of the LORD came back a second time and touched him and said, 'Get up and eat, for the journey is too much for you.'" Elijah partook again of that heaven-provided food and was strengthened . . . enabled to travel for forty days and forty nights (!) "until he reached Horeb, the mountain of God" (verse 8). There were many times on my cancer journey when I lost my physical appetite due to the harsh chemotherapy treatments. But I am forever thankful that I never lost my spiritual appetite. Spiritual food and water strengthened me time and again when I had had enough . . . when the journey was too much for me. Maybe, like Elijah, you've had enough and even told God you want to die. I encourage you not to give up, but to cry out to God and read the Bible. God knows when the journey is too much for us. He is our provider, the one who can miraculously provide for us . . . anytime, anywhere—even in the deserts of our lives. I now know that heaven-provided spiritual "desert" food can be the best tasting, most satisfying food of all, strengthening us for the journey ahead. Remember Elijah and his journey to Horeb. Strengthened and encouraged, he went on! You can, too . . . one day at a time. Just one day at a time.

Cast your burden on the LORD,

and he will sustain you;

he will never permit the righteous to be moved.

(Psalm 55:22, NRSV)

CARRYING A HEAVY LOAD?

After casting a particular burden on the Lord one morning, I recalled a certain memory. Years ago, the day after 9/11, I attended a prayer service. Although that service was inspirational and encouraging, I still felt a deep sadness as my family and I walked to our car that night. The horrible events of the day before remained on my mind. On the way to our car, we saw a little boy walking with his diaper bag slung around his neck. That diaper bag was so heavy that he kept stumbling over it. His daddy tried to help by taking the diaper bag, but the child protested. He was determined to carry that heavy load himself! As we passed them, my husband smiled and said, "That's a pretty heavy load for a little guy." And the daddy answered, "He wants to carry it." Those words stayed with me; and back at our car, God revealed to me that I had been hanging onto my burdens, my sadness, my grief over the events of September 11th. Just as that little boy needed to give his heavy load to his daddy, I needed to give my heavy burdens to my heavenly Father. For my heavenly Father, just like that little boy's daddy, was reaching down and longing to help. Have you, too, been carrying a heavy load all by yourself? You can choose to cast that burden on the Lord today. He is reaching down . . . longing to help. "Cast your burden on the LORD, and he will sustain you; he will never permit the righteous to be moved."

But the Lord stood at my side

and gave me strength.

(2 Timothy 4:17)

STRENGTH CAN BE YOURS

If you're feeling weak and beaten down by difficult circumstances, I have three verses to share with you.

2 Timothy 4:17 - But the Lord stood at my side and gave me strength.

During my first cancer journey, there were times I was so sick and so weak that all I could utter in prayer was one word: "Help!" In response to that desperate, simple cry, the Lord would draw near and strengthen me to go on. Be encouraged! The Lord can stand at your side and give you the needed strength to go on.

1 Samuel 23:16 - And Saul's son Jonathan went to David at Horesh and helped him find strength in God.

Just as Jonathan went to David and helped him find strength in God, God sent people to help me find strength in him amidst the rigors of chemotherapy. Papa Don, my friend's dad, was one of them. He came alongside me early on in my cancer journey and was there each step of the way. I would often wake up at the hospital and find him sitting in a chair by my bed and praying for me. Be encouraged! God can send others to help you find strength in him.

1 Samuel 30:6, NKJV - But David strengthened himself in the LORD his God.

On my cancer journey, I strengthened myself in the Lord through spending time in prayer, reading and studying the Bible—even wearing out one copy, claiming promises God had given me for my circumstances, and singing praise and worship songs. Be encouraged! You can strengthen yourself in the Lord your God when you draw near to him through prayer, his Word, singing and more. There are all kinds of things that can rob us of strength: affliction, sorrow, not eating properly, lack of sleep, unconfessed sin, and many others too numerous to list. Psalm 29:11 tells us that "the LORD gives strength to his people." And as Philippians 4:13 tells us, "I can do all things through Him who strengthens me" (NASB). Through him, I was enabled to endure four cancers . . . through his strength . . . one day at a time. May you be strengthened today, either through the Lord standing at your side and giving you strength, or through others helping you find your strength in him, or through strengthening yourself in the Lord by spending time in prayer and his Word. Be strong in him—*in him*—today! We were never meant to go it alone.

*S*et me free from my prison,

that I may praise your name.

(Psalm 142:7)

SET FREE

Psalm 142 was written by David while he hid from Saul in a cave—a cave that felt like a prison to him. After telling the Lord his troubles, David made a request of the Lord in verse 7: "Set me free from my prison, that I may praise your name." David believed that God could set him free from his prison, and he asked him to do that for him. Considering the word *prison*, we can turn to Acts 12, where we find Peter jailed and then miraculously freed. In verse 17, upon his release and while speaking to the believers, Peter "described how the Lord had brought him out of prison." Early on in my cancer journey, I felt like a prisoner myself . . . imprisoned by my trial, my attitude, fear, loneliness and the like. However, just as he did for David and Peter, God set me free! He also set Paul and Silas free in Acts 16. Maybe you remember the story. Paul and Silas were wrongly accused and thrown into prison, but chose to praise God regardless of their circumstances! In verse 26, we find the result of their praise, "Suddenly there was such a violent earthquake that the foundations of the prison were shaken. At once all the prison doors flew open, and everyone's chains came loose." Did you catch that? Not just their own chains came loose, but everyone's did! One thing is clear . . . the Lord can deliver us from prison! Are you feeling imprisoned today? If so, do as David did; believe that the Lord can set you free, and ask him to do just that. Also choose to praise the Lord as Paul and Silas did while locked in a jail cell with their feet fastened in stocks. Prayer and praise can set the captives free! What if your deliverance doesn't happen overnight, though? Keep praying. And keep praising God! Praise has a way of setting us free (internally), even when the prison doors of circumstances remain locked (externally). That I know. Remember . . . your praise may even result in other captives being set free, just like what happened in Acts 16!

"In this world you will have trouble.

But take heart! I have overcome the world."

(John 16:33)

THE BEST IS YET TO COME!

I remember the week that my dear friend's aunt Dot passed away and I found out that a woman from our church had been given six months to live. While thinking about both of those difficult circumstances, I was reminded of Jesus' words in John 16:33. How often that verse strengthened me in the middle of my own trials . . . reminding me that, for believers in Jesus, the best is yet to come! What else does God's Word have to say about suffering? Here's a glimpse:

2 Corinthians 4:17 - For our light and momentary troubles are achieving for us an eternal glory that far outweighs them all.

2 Corinthians 12:9 - But he said to me, "My grace is sufficient for you, for my power is made perfect in weakness." Therefore I will boast all the more gladly about my weaknesses, so that Christ's power may rest on me.

Romans 5:3–4 - Not only so, but we also glory in our sufferings, because we know that suffering produces perseverance; perseverance, character; and character, hope.

2 Corinthians 4:11 - For we who are alive are always being given over to death for Jesus' sake, so that his life may also be revealed in our mortal body.

Romans 8:28 - And we know that in all things God works for the good of those who love him, who have been called according to his purpose.

I certainly don't have all the answers regarding suffering; but I do know, from personal experience, there is much to be learned within the crucible of suffering when we turn to God, seek him through prayer and his Word, and trust him through it all. I also know that God may accomplish things through our suffering that never would have been accomplished apart from it. When confronted by suffering, I choose to focus on God and his higher purposes. I have found that focusing on suffering brings despair, self-pity and fear; but focusing on God fills me with hope and strength. And that hope and strength enable me to go on, one day at a time, until that day when God will wipe every tear from my eyes, and "'there will be no more death' or mourning or crying or pain, for the old order of things has passed away" (Revelation 21:4). If you are a suffering child of God, I encourage you to pray, read the Bible, ask God for his perspective, obey him and trust him . . . all the way . . . home! Home! This world is not our home. The best is yet to come!

"Do not harden your hearts as you did in the rebellion, during the time of testing in the wilderness, where your ancestors tested and tried me."

(Hebrews 3:8–9)

BEHAVIORS THAT TEST GOD

On one particular day, these words stood out to me from Hebrews 3:8–9: "during the time of testing in the wilderness, where your ancestors tested and tried me." After reading those words in Hebrews, I was reminded that God tests us and that our behaviors can test and try God! Turning to the Exodus story (to which those Hebrews verses refer), I find God testing his people. I also find God's people testing him. At the waters of Marah and Elim, instead of trusting God for provision, the people grumbled. In the Desert of Sin, while longing for the food of Egypt, the people grumbled again; and when they did, Moses told them that they weren't grumbling against him and against Aaron, but against the Lord. At Rephidim there wasn't any water to drink; and after the Israelites argued with Moses about it, he asked them, "Why do you quarrel with me? Why do you put the LORD to the test?" (Exodus 17:2). At Horeb they also tested the Lord when they asked, "Is the LORD among us or not?" (Exodus 17:7). And they asked that question again after witnessing God's miraculous parting of the Red Sea, after his provision of heavenly manna, and on and on. In Exodus 32, we find the people worshipping an idol instead of the one true God, and that behavior roused the Lord's anger. The Israelites tested God through their unbelief. And that unbelief led to grumbling, quarreling, not accepting their God-appointed circumstances, worshipping an idol . . . disobeying God! Have you ever considered the fact that you might be testing God by your behaviors and attitudes within the time of his testing in your life? The Israelites tested God. The results? They wandered in the desert for forty years, and only two of the men from the large group who could have been allowed to enter the promised land ever actually entered it. Yes, God tests us, but let's not test him! *Our* promised land is waiting . . .

Let him who walks in darkness and has no light
trust in the name of the LORD and rely on his God.
(Isaiah 50:10, ESV)

WALKING IN THE DARK?

For any children of God who feel as if they're walking in the dark, without any light, Isaiah 50:10 offers instruction. The first instruction from Isaiah is to "trust in the name of the LORD." God has many names in Scripture, and his names reveal who he is. The following are some of God's names: El Roi (The God Who Sees), El Shaddai (The All-Sufficient One), Jehovah Jireh (The Lord Will Provide), Jehovah Rapha (The Lord Who Heals) and Jehovah Raah (The Lord My Shepherd). If you are walking in the dark, choose to trust in the name of the Lord (in who he is). The second instruction from Isaiah, for the children of God who feel as if they're walking in the dark, without any light, is to rely on God. According to the *Hebrew-Greek Key Word Study Bible*, the Hebrew word translated *rely* in that verse can also be translated "lean, lie, rest or stay." Got the picture? If you are walking in the dark, choose to rely on God. There were times during my first cancer when heaven seemed silent and God's face hidden. At times I truly felt as if I *were* walking in the dark, without any light. But with God's help, I chose to trust in his name—in who he is—and to rely on him. Eventually the light shone through. By then I knew God in a deeper way, and I also knew that he was all I needed. When times are hard and you feel as if you're walking in the dark, without any light, remember Isaiah's instructions . . . to trust in the name of the Lord and rely on God. God is faithful to his children. And one day, light will break through your darkness . . . no matter how dark that darkness has been! In the meantime, don't waste the dark. Don't waste the dark. The best is yet to come . . .

Turn to me and be gracious to me,

for I am lonely and afflicted.

(Psalm 25:16)

LONELY?

There are days when I choose to read a psalm or proverb that corresponds with the date. For example, on the 25th of any month, I can read Psalm 25. Tucked within that Psalm are the following words, found in verse 16: "Turn to me and be gracious to me, for I am lonely and afflicted." After my mother-in-law passed away, one of her friends told us that she had been lonely. At times, we had sensed her loneliness, and I used to think to myself, *If only she knew Jesus!* However, she had long refused to enter into a saving relationship with him (until, that is, just days before she passed). For months, during my first cancer, I basically lived in isolation due to a compromised white count—a result of the harsh chemotherapy treatments. Was I lonely back then? Yes, there were some lonely days for me during that time—but, thankfully, not many! Why? Because of Jesus! Daily I chose to draw near to him through praying often and feasting on the words of Scripture. One of the results of my drawing near to Jesus at that time was that he drew near to me, and any loneliness was sent packing! How about you? Are you lonely today? If so, why not turn the psalmist's prayer into your own prayer? "Turn to me and be gracious to me, for I am lonely and afflicted." Then draw near to Jesus through prayer and Scripture reading. Luke 5:16 tells us that "Jesus often withdrew to lonely places and prayed." A lonely place can become a place of prayer. Just as it was for Jesus . . . and for me. May your lonely place become a place of prayer . . . today and every day!

*May your roots go down deep
into the soil of God's marvelous love.
(Ephesians 3:17, TLB)*

GOD'S MARVELOUS LOVE

Years ago, during trying times, a friend gave me a Bible. Through the pages of that book, she had highlighted numerous helpful verses for me. One of those highlighted verses was this: "May your roots go down deep into the soil of God's marvelous love." The longer I live, the more I realize how crucial it is for our roots to go down deep into God's love. Without deep roots into God's love we'll never know true happiness; and we'll also more easily have our faith uprooted when the storms of life come . . . rather than standing firm in God and his great love for us. As a child, I grew up with that old saying about boys: *He loves me, he loves me not. He loves me, he loves me not.* Remembering that saying, I realize now it could never be said about God, for God's love is unfailing. And nothing can ever separate God's children from his love (see Romans 8:38–39). If you don't yet know that God loves you, consider the meaning of the cross. It's the place where a holy God took on our sins and died so that we might be forgiven and inherit eternal life. If you're still unsure of God's love for you, even after reflecting on what Jesus did on the cross, ask God to give you insight into his love. Years ago I needed a reminder myself of how much God loved me; so I asked God to reveal his love for me anew . . . and he did, in a tangible and tender way. God's love for you and me is so great it surpasses our understanding . . . we'll never fully comprehend it this side of heaven . . . but we can know it in part. God loves you! God loves you! He loves you! Remind yourself of that truth often, even saying it aloud, so that your roots "go down deep into the soil of God's marvelous love." That's the kind of soil that produces the best and strongest roots . . . for life . . . abundant life!

Satisfy us in the morning with your unfailing love,

that we may sing for joy and be glad all our days.

(Psalm 90:14)

UNFAILING LOVE

According to the Bible, God's love is marvelous, perfect, great, unfailing, everlasting and more. God's love is also unconditional, which means it is not dependent upon what we do or fail to do. We will never fully comprehend God's love for us, and nothing can ever separate us from that love. But the trials of our lives can make us forget how very much God loves us! If you're going through a trial today, I encourage you to ponder anew God's great love for you. Here are some verses to contemplate as you get started:

Lamentations 3:22 - Because of the LORD's great love we are not consumed, for his compassions never fail.

1 John 4:18 - There is no fear in love. But perfect love drives out fear.

1 John 4:9–10 - This is how God showed his love among us: He sent his one and only Son into the world that we might live through him. This is love: not that we loved God, but that he loved us and sent his Son as an atoning sacrifice for our sins.

Romans 8:38–39 - I am convinced that neither death nor life, neither angels nor demons, neither the present nor the future, nor any powers, neither height nor depth, nor anything else in all creation, will be able to separate us from the love of God that is in Christ Jesus our Lord.

Psalm 108:4 - Great is your love, higher than the heavens; your faithfulness reaches to the skies.

Psalm 118:1 - His love endures forever.

Proverbs 19:22 tells us this: "What a person desires is unfailing love." And God's love is an unfailing love . . . a love that was so powerfully demonstrated at the cross. Yes, God loves you! He loves you indeed! May his love fall fresh on you today.

AFTERWORD

The world around us tries to seduce us to put our hope in the things of this world . . . temporary things such as your health, finances, doctor, education, family, exercise regimen, diet and more. Things that are temporary can offer only temporary hope, though.

In 1991 I was given a five percent chance of surviving five years. Amidst that consuming fire, I could have put my hope in the things of this world such as my doctor or a treatment plan or a diet; yet none of those things could ever have given me lasting hope.

Thankfully, back then God began to draw me, with cords of love, to his Son Jesus. Eventually I came to the foot of the cross, fearful, desperate, empty and broken . . . without hope, peace or joy. There at the cross I surrendered my life, my dreams and my all to God. I repented of my sins and trusted in Jesus alone for my ultimate destiny. When I did that, God forgave me of my sins, and new life and abiding hope sprang up within me. Peace and joy overflowed. My life forever changed that day!

I have endured and survived many fiery trials in my life. Some of those trials have been big; others have been small. Some have lasted a long time, but others a short while. Not only have my trials varied, but so have my responses to them. For example, my mom died when I was only twenty-seven years old. I initially cried out to the God I had learned about during my childhood Sunday school days. Yet soon after, my own pride convinced me to depend on myself for healing. But the hurt ran deep, and what I really needed was God's healing touch.

Years later, at age thirty-three and diagnosed with stage-four ovarian cancer, I again initially cried out to God while at the same time depending on my own strength to see me through. Weeks later, amidst intense and grueling chemotherapy, I was brought to the end of myself . . . and eventually chose to depend on God.

Back when I relied on my own strength, during the fires of my life my days were marked by constant worry, overwhelming despair and, at times, consuming fear. But after coming to know Jesus, my days have been characterized by a supernatural peace, abundant joy and abiding hope, even during times of suffering.

So what about you? Are you enduring a personal fire? If so, will you choose a temporary hope by putting your confidence in the things of this world? Or will you choose an abiding hope, which is enduring, steadfast and continuing without change—a hope that comes through a relationship with Jesus? The choice you make will determine not only the quality of your days, but your eternal destiny.

I am forever thankful I chose to put my faith in Jesus during the fieriest trial of my life. Nothing can ever compare to the hope, peace, joy, contentment, meaning, purpose, eternal security and more that are mine in him. He has seen me through the fire and will see me through any future fires. Fires cannot quench the abiding hope that is now mine—my hope will remain, for its source is not of this world.

Yes, fiery trials will enter our lives this side of heaven, but there is hope. Always hope . . . in Jesus. Jesus. He is the hope of the entire world. And with Jesus beside us, the flames will not consume us . . . even when they rage . . . even if they include a shocking diagnosis of a five percent chance of surviving five years . . . or . . . _____ (you fill in the blank).

My prayer for you is found in Ephesians 1:18, that "the eyes of your heart may be enlightened in order that you may know the hope to which he has called you." The kind of hope that endures . . . abiding hope.

"For I know the plans I have for you,"

declares the LORD, "plans to prosper you

and not to harm you,

plans to give you hope and a future."

(Jeremiah 29:11)

ACKNOWLEDGEMENTS

Brett and Sheila Waldman and TRISTAN Publishing—What a joy-filled adventure it has been walking this road with you! Thank you for believing in me, encouraging me and for all of the prayers, labor and love you poured into this project. You bring joy to the Father's heart . . . and mine.

Renee Garrick—You have such amazing discernment and attention to detail when it comes to editing and proofreading. Thank you for all that you have done!

Pete and Zach—Thank you for all of your steadfast prayers and encouragement throughout this project. You bring such joy to my heart and my days! Keep following Him. I love you tons.

Pastor Troy—Thank you for being a pastor who passionately loves Jesus, unashamedly speaks God's truth and shepherds his flock with love and grace. We are so very grateful that you are our pastor! Thank you for all you are and do.

Pastor Peter—You were there at the start of this project. Thank you for your time and encouragement. God's plan was bigger than mine, and he used you to help guide me to it.

Kelly McClintock, Wendy Nachreiner and Kerry Teel—Thank you for all of your weekly encouragement and prayers for this book and more. Jesus shines through each of you. Keep living for Him!

Trail Mix community—Your love, prayer support, encouragement, fellowship and more has made our lives richer this side of heaven. Thank you. We love you and are so grateful God crossed our paths with yours.

Thank you to all who have cheered me on and prayed for me regarding this project. You know who you are. You bless my life more than you will ever know!

My Heavenly Father—In the words of King David, "Who am I, Sovereign Lord, and what is my family, that you have brought me this far?" (2 Samuel 7:18). Thank you and praise you for all that you have done! The glory belongs to you. The One for whom nothing is impossible!

For additional encouragement and blessing,

be sure to check out

www.TRISTANpublishing.com/books

and click on Abiding Hope!